CountryMusic ★ Stars

CARRIE UNDERWOOD

By Adele Newroad

Gareth Stevens Publishing

Please visit our Web site www.garethstevens.com. For a free color catalog of all our high-quality books, call toll free 1-800-542-2595 or fax 1-877-542-2596.

Library of Congress Cataloging-in-Publication Data

Newroad, Adele.
 Carrie Underwood / Adele Newroad.
    p. cm. — (Country music stars)
 Includes index.
 ISBN 978-1-4339-3602-9 (pbk.)
 ISBN 978-1-4339-3603-6 (6-pack)
 ISBN 978-1-4339-3601-2 (library binding)
 1. Underwood, Carrie, 1983—Juvenile literature. 2. Singers—United States—Biography—Juvenile literature. I. Title.
 ML3930.U53N49 2010
 782.421642092—dc22
 [B]

2009040598

Published in 2010 by Gareth Stevens Publishing
111 East 14th Street, Suite 349
New York, NY 10003

Copyright © 2010 Gareth Stevens Publishing

Designer: Michael J. Flynn
Editor: Therese Shea

Photo credits: Cover (Carrie Underwood), pp. 1, 21, 29 © Ethan Miller/Getty Images; cover (background) Shutterstock.com; pp. 5, 11, 13, 15, 27 © Kevin Winter/Getty Images; p. 7 © Tony R. Phipps/WireImage/Getty Images; p. 9 © Ray Mickshaw/WireImage/Getty Images; p. 17 © MLB Photos via Getty Images/Getty Images; p. 19 © John Sciulli/WireImage/Getty Images; p. 23 © Frank Micelotta/ACMA/Getty Images; p. 25 © Eric Charbonneau/WireImage/Getty Images.

Printed in the United States of America

CPSIA compliance information: Batch #CW10GS: For further information contact Gareth Stevens, New York, New York at 1-800-542-2595.

CONTENTS

A COUNTRY GIRL

Carrie Underwood is a country music singer. A TV show made her famous.

Carrie was born in Oklahoma in 1983. She lived on a farm with her parents.

Carrie was a good student. She was a good singer, too.

AMERICAN IDOL

Carrie heard about tryouts for

American Idol. She got on the show!

Many singers competed for the prize.

Carrie sang well week after week.

Carrie

13

Many people thought Carrie sang
best. She won the prize!

FAMOUS SINGER

Carrie became very famous. People wanted to hear her sing.

Carrie's first album came out in 2005.

She won many awards for it.

19

In 2006, Carrie went on tour with other country stars. Here she is with Brad Paisley.

Carrie made another album in 2007.

People loved this album, too!

23

SPECIAL SONGS

In 2007, Carrie sang a song for a movie called *Enchanted.* The song is called "Ever, Ever After."

Carrie writes some of her own songs.

She writes about love and having fun.

A BIG AWARD

Carrie was named Entertainer of the Year in 2009. What will she do next?

TIMELINE

1983 Carrie Underwood is born in Oklahoma.

2005 Carrie wins *American Idol.*

2005 Carrie's first album comes out.

2006 Carrie goes on tour.

2007 Carrie's second album comes out.

2007 Carrie sings a song for the movie *Enchanted.*

2009 Carrie is named Entertainer of the Year.

FOR MORE INFORMATION

Books:

La Bella, Laura. *Carrie Underwood.* New York: Rosen
Publishing, 2008.

Marcovitz, Hal. *Carrie Underwood.* Broomall, PA: Mason
Crest Publishers, 2010.

Tieck, Sarah. *Carrie Underwood.* Edina, MN: ABDO
Publishing, 2008.

Web Sites:

Arista Nashville: Carrie Underwood

www.aristanashville.com/artists/details.cfm?artistid=1000011

The Official Carrie Underwood Site

www.carrieunderwoodofficial.com/

GLOSSARY

award: a prize given to someone for doing something well

compete: to try to win a contest

entertainer: a person who acts, sings, dances, or plays music for other people

tour: a trip to many places in order to entertain people

tryout: a test of someone's talent

INDEX